UNDERSTANDING EACH OTHER

A Guide for Parents and their Children

In all thy getting get an understanding.
Proverbs 4:7

Dr. Grace LaJoy Henderson

Inspirations by Grace LaJoy
Raymore, MO 64083
www.gracelajoy.com

Understanding Each Other   Dr. Grace LaJoy Henderson
A Guide for Parents and their Children

The content of this book is a result of real responses from actual children and parents. Names have been withheld in order to maintain the privacy of the respondents. Understanding Each Other is published for your information and enjoyment and should not be used in lieu of professional family counseling.

Eagle logo by Darlene L. Thompson-Williams for Grace LaJoy Henderson. Cover by Grace LaJoy Henderson

UNDERSTAND EACH OTHER: *A Guide for Parents and their Children*
Copyright © 2008 by Grace LaJoy Henderson
Published by Inspirations by Grace LaJoy
Raymore, MO 64083
www.gracelajoy.com

Library of Congress Control Number: 2008922302

ISBN 978-0-9814607-0-3

Printed in the United States of America

Table of Contents

Understanding Each Other
A Guide for Parents and their Children

Dr. Grace LaJoy Henderson

FOREWORD

There is no one manual with all the answers to parenting. Although there are several resources available to guide us, each parent-child relationship is different. What may be suitable for one relationship may not be suitable for others.

Understanding ourselves will equip us to better understand others specifically our offspring. Many times as parents we do not want our children to make the same mistakes that we made.

I believe that all parents want their children to have a better life than themselves, which causes us as parents to sometimes become overbearing and untrusting in our offspring. This inhibits us from building solid relationships with our children and creates walls of defense which can become difficult to tear down when it comes to our loved ones.

I have found in my seventeen years of being a parent that if I train my child to always acknowledge God, if I lead by example, make my expectations' clear, and I do not let on that I am or my life is perfect, but allow my child the chance to grow, it will lead to a very healthy relationship and will produce a productive citizen within society.

Unwavering love is the key, but rules and boundaries are also very important. If no relationship exists then communication between parent and child will be difficult. Everyone needs a place of refuge; and someone they can trust.

It has been written that "in all thy getting get an understanding". The best way to guarantee a good understanding is to keep the lines of communication open leaving no room for assumption, what better way to understand each other than through constructive communication.

What may be acceptable in one family may not be acceptable in another family; but as long as there is open and respectful communication there will always be a level of trust and understanding.

Andrea Tribitt, Gospel Artist
Sounds of Blackness

As an educator in the public school system for eight years, Andrea Tribitt has hands-on influence with today's youth and uses her singing as a way to draw them in. She has shared her music ministry with millions of people inside and outside of the United States, including singing at the White House in Washington, DC.

THE PURPOSE OF THIS BOOK

The purpose of this book is to help parents and children to understand each other better. How? Well, we asked the same question of 100 people... 50 parents ages 24 through 80 and 50 children ages 5 through 53.

We asked the *parents*: "If you could get your child(ren) to understand just one thing about you, what would that one thing be?" Then, we asked the *children*: "If you could get your parents to understand just one thing about you, what would that one thing be?"

We compiled the responses into this book and are now making this book available to parents and children of all ages so that they may be educated, as well as encouraged, by the responses that have been gathered.

The responses were gathered from working adults, church going children and adults, non-church going children and adults, college students, and various other individuals.

INTRODUCTION

There are resources for parents and there are resources for children. However, *Understanding Each Other* is unique because it is a resource for both parents *and* children. It actually gives both parents and their children the opportunity to share their feelings as well as learn what the other feels.

Regardless of how old we are, we need to be understood by our parents and our children. As a result of reading this book, parents and their children will know that many other people share the same feeling, thoughts, emotions, and needs as they do.

Understanding Each Other allows both parents and children to communicate openly about issues that are often times unintentionally ignored as we go through our life sincerely trying to obtain and maintain family cohesiveness.

Understanding Each Other
A Guide for Parents and their Children

Dr. Grace LaJoy Henderson

ABOUT THE RESPONSES
A word from the author

Although a few people came up with a response right away, I found that most people to whom I asked the question needed time to *think* about their answer. This is not the type of question that most people think about everyday.

Many people were happy to give a response because it allowed them a moment to reflect on what *they* wanted someone to understand about *them.*

I was impressed with the maturity of the children's responses and the sincerity of the adult's. I was impressed with the few parents in their 70's and 80's who reported that they have a very understanding relationship with their children. I feel that this is because their children are older now and have come to appreciate and respect their parents for who they are as persons and no longer only see them as "parents". Many of them have their own children now and have learned to appreciate parenthood.

I found that the elderly have as many needs as the younger people. Even the adults in the 25-50 age range, who have families of their own, still desire for *their own* parents to understand them.

I realized, by conducting this project, that the question that was asked is a very personal one. The question caused the respondents to "open up" in order to answer honestly. I really appreciate everyone who took the time to answer.

The responses have not been edited and appear in the exact words of the respondents. The honesty and the "realness" of these responses will educate and encourage you!

If you could get your

child(ren) to understand just

one thing about you, what

would that one thing be?

Understanding Each Other
A Guide for Parents and their Children

Dr. Grace LaJoy Henderson

Age 24

I would like for my children to understand that as a first time parent, I do not know everything about parenting; I am doing my best. There is a reason why I say everything that I say and do.

Age 24

I would like for my children to understand my personality. How I think. The reasons why I do what I do. How I feel about certain things.

Age 24

I would like for my children to understand that when I say I am tired, leave me alone!!

Age 24

I would like for my children to understand that I have a great deal of perseverance and determina-tion, which I try to instill in them. So, what seems like anger with them, is actually disappointment in

myself for not showing them properly what to do.

Age 24

I would like for my children to understand that I

mean business!!

Age 28

I would like for my children to understand that I

must show kindness and compassion to others,

regardless of their race, education, economics

status, background, etc. I would like for them to

follow my footsteps and treat others with the same

kindness and compassion.

Age 28

I would like for my children to understand that the

reason why I discipline them is to correct them.

Age 30

I would like for my children to understand that I love them regardless of how good or bad they act. I love them regardless of how angry I get at them sometimes. I love them just as much when I am mad as I do when I am happy.

Age 30

I would like for my child to understand moral values. That I must instill the right moral values in her.

Age 30

I would like for my children to understand that when I give them advice, it is for their own good. I am not trying to hurt them or keep them from having fun.

Age 32

I would like for my children to understand that I love them.

Age 34

I would like for my children to understand that the reason why I encourage them to try so many things, such as piano lessons, ballet, singing, and etc. is because I want them to have opportunities that I did not have. I want them to have many experiences so that they will have plenty to choose from in order to make a decision for themselves about what they want to stick with.

Age 34

I would like for my children to understand that education is very important. Although it may not seem important <u>now</u> it will benefit them in the long run.

Age 35

I would like for my children to understand who I am today. Because I am a minister, I have to be a help to more people that just my child and I really need for my child to understand this.

Age 35

I would like for my children to understand why I make and enforce the rules that I make. I feel that these rules are important because I do not want them to go through the same things that I went through. I make these rules as an attempt to prevent them from making the same mistakes that I made.

Age 35

I would like for my children to understand that I am not perfect. I am not always right just because I am the parent. I do strive to set a good example for them.

Age 35

I would like for my son to understand why I get so angry at him when he does certain things. Why I get so irritated. I have not adjusted to dealing with kids yet, although one would think that I have since I am a parent. I have done things in front of my son that I should not have done. I have messed up and made many mistakes with him, but, I see my mistakes now and am trying to do right by him because he is very important to me.

Age 36

I would like for my daughter to understand the unconditional love that I have for her.

Age 37

I would like for my children to understand that I only check up on them a lot because I care. They are still children. No matter how old they get they

Are still my children, so I would like for them to

allow me to check up on them and know that I am

only checking up on them because I care.

Age 37

I would like for my son to understand that I am a

God-fearing mother and I have always tried to instill

Godly principles in him.

Age 37

I would like for my children to understand that they

must do what I say.

Age 38

I would like for my children to understand my

remarriage. They do not have to be jealous of

another individual in my life because my love for

them will never change.

Age 38

I would like for my daughter to understand why it is

so important that I care about other people. This is

one of the main commandments (Love thy neighbor

as thyself); The art of reaping what you sow. I want

her to know about love: If we do not give love out,

we do not get it back in return. I want her to see me

following those examples of Christ and for her to

follow those same examples.

Age 39

I would like for my son to understand that even

though I fuss at him, I want him to be the best that

he can be. I want him to strive for perfection.

When he messes up, I am going to be tough on him

in order to help him to straighten up.

Age 40

I would like for my step children to understand as a step parent, I do a lot of caring things for them. I would like for them to respect me as a mother because I do many things for them that a mother would do (wash their clothes, feed them, etc.)

Age 42

I would like for my children to understand that the reason why I am so tough on them is because I love them and to prepare them to be successful in the world.

Age 43

I want my children to understand that I am a "changed" woman. (my belief in God)

Age 44

I would like for my children to understand that my intentions and aim are to get them to be the best that they can be; not for <u>my</u> sake but for <u>their</u> sake.

Age 44

I would like for my children to understand how much I really love the Lord

Age 45

I want my daughter to understand that I am on her side and anything that I do and/or tell her is for her good.

Age 47

I would like for my children to understand that I love them.

Age 48

I would like for my children to understand my love for them. They think I am mean but I love them unconditionally.

Age 48

I want my children to understand that I am saved, and that I believe in Jesus Christ and nothing else.

Age 49

My kids really understand me more than I realize.

Age 50

I want my son to understand that I mean him well. Anything that I say to him is for his benefit.

Age 50

I would like for my children to understand that I love them. That I discipline them because I love them.

Age 52

I would like for my children to understand my faith in the Lord; and with the Lord's help, we will make it through difficult situations.

Age 53

I would like for my children to understand that my personal decisions are made with information that they are not always aware of.

Age 57

I would like for my children to understand that I always have their best interest at heart. I speak to them from experience. It is not always what they want to hear, but it is what they need to hear in order to keep them from making the same mistakes that I made.

Age 50+ (would not disclose age)

I would like for my children to understand that I mean what I say!!

Age 50+ (would not disclose age)

I would like for my children to understand that the reason why I fuss is because I am concerned about them. I am concerned about whether they are going in the right direction. Whenever I notice them straying away from the right direction I fuss. I want them to know that I care about them.

Age 67

I want my children to understand my comfort zone. That it is different from theirs. What I *have* is what I *need*. I only buy things that I *need* even though I have the money to buy more. I do not spend more that I *need* to spend even though I can afford to spend more.

Age 68

I would like for my daughter to understand that she can depend on me as a father. She can come to me with problems and ask me for whatever she wants.

Age 69

I would like for my children to understand that I do want to hear from them. I am interested enough in them that I want them to keep in touch whether by telephone, letter, or *something*, just keep in touch!! If they are sick, I want to know. If they are going on vacation, I want to know about it. I am interested in their lives.

Age 71

I would like for my children to understand that I believe that there is one God regardless of religion and that nothing last but "right". I will knock them in the head regardless of their age.

Age 73

There is not anything that I need for my child to understand about me. He is grown now; he is not a kid anymore.

Age 75

My children know me pretty well; we have a good understanding. We talk about most things and they know how I think.

Age 80

I would like for my children to understand that I have always been their provider; whatever they needed I provided it for them.

Age 80

I feel that my children already understand everything about me. They love, respect, and honor me for who I am.

If you could get your

<u>parents</u> to understand just *one*

thing about you, what would

that one thing be?

Understanding Each Other
A Guide for Parents and their Children

Dr. Grace LaJoy Henderson

Age 5

I would like for my parents to understand… "Don't spank me".

Age 6

I would like for my parents to understand that when I am grown up I need to get out by myself; because I am going to be a grown up soon.

Age 7

I would like for my parents to understand that when I am grown up I am not going to be alone; I am going to be with Jesus.

Age 9

I would like for my parents to understand slang words. When I say slang words my parents never know what they mean. I would like for my parents to understand the meaning of my slang words.

Age 10

I would like for my parents to understand that I do not give up very easily. If I am trying to do something (like pass a test at school) I am very determined to do it.

Age 10

I would like for my parents to understand how I feel about them. The way I feel about them is like loving them every day. It's like when someone hurts my feelings, they will try to cheer me up. Whenever I hurt myself on something, they put a band-aid on my pain.

Age 10

I would like for my parents to understand how confident I am about all things. For example: If I want to start my own company or business I am confident that I can do it.

Dr. Grace LaJoy Henderson

Age 10

I would like for my parents to understand that they do not have to always give me the things that I want. Sometimes they give me the things that I want when I do not have the things that I need.

Age 11

I would like for my parents to understand that I want to hang out with my friends. She likes for me to stay home and keep her company. If she knew how hard it was to make friends, I think she would understand how I feel.

Age 11

I would like for my parents to understand how lonely I am.

Age 12

I would like for my parents to understand I am growing up, and it is not time to let go, but it is time to loosen the grip. I feel that my mother can trust me and I feel that I have proved myself responsible enough to handle some difficult situations on my own. I can not be living under my mother's roof until I am forty. I need to learn now how to take responsibility for my own actions; how to be myself; be on my own a little bit. What I am basically saying is…I guess I'm growing up.

Age 12

I would like for my parents to understand that it is okay for a girl to go with a boy and <u>not</u> kiss or have sex.

Age 13

I would like my mother to understand my talking to boys that she doesn't know, because she is not going to know every boy that I meet. Also, I want my mother to let me go over to more of my friends' houses.

Age 13

I want my mother to know that I am responsible enough to go places with boys (not home) and I know what to do and what not to do. I want her to let me have boyfriends; I mean I have one, but she does not seem to understand that sometimes my relationship is serious, and the one I just got out of was for seven months and it was pretty serious.

Age 13

I would like for my parents to understand that I think I am old enough to talk to boys and that I can talk on the phone until about 11:30pm. I would also want to be able to go places with boys because I am responsible enough to know what's right and wrong.

Age 13

I would like for my parents to understand what is happening in my life; at school, and etc.

Age 14

I would like for my parents to understand that I am not perfect.

Age 15

I would like for my parents to understand that I am trying to do my best. I would like for my parents to help me when I can't do my best.

Age 15

I would like for my parents to understand that I need them to respect my space and treat me the age that I am.

Age 15

I would like for my parents to understand that I am not perfect

Age 15

I would like for my parents to understand the way I think about education.

Age 16

I would like for my parents to understand that I can be responsible in any situation. For example: watching my sister and brother when she is not home.

Age 17

I would like for my parents to understand that I need my own privacy and she does not have to check on everything I do.

Age 17

I would like for my parents to understand that cash rules everything around me.

Age 18

I would like for my parents to understand that I am young and I want to have fun at the time. That is why I am always gone.

Age 20

I would like for my parents to understand that I am 20 and not 12. So, treat me like an adult. Also, I do not like having curfews.

Age 24

The thing I wish my parents would understand about me is that just because I don't always do the things that they believe to be the best for me does not mean that I don't listen to them and appreciate the advice they give me.

Age 24

I would like for my parents to understand that my love for them is strong despite our lack of communication.

Age 24

I would like for my parents to understand that I try to be my best.

Age 26

I would like for my parents to understand that I am a conqueror and I don't give up. I have faith and patience.

Age 28

I would like for my parents to understand that sometimes I need time alone just to think about what direction in life that God wants me to follow. I appreciate their advice, but I need space to know what I want. I want them to trust me to go the right way.

Age 30

I would like for my parents to understand how understanding I am.

Age 30

I would like for my parents to understand that even though I do not do everything that they suggest, I still listen and take it to heart. It may appear as though I am not listening when they give me words of wisdom, but I am indeed listening and I appreciate everything that they say to me.

Age 30

Though my father has died, I would like for him to understand that I appreciate the way he spent time talking to me (sharing his wisdom). Instead of always using his belt when I acted up, he spent time talking to me. As a result, I am able to share his wisdom with others. Though he is gone, his wisdom lives on.

Age 31

I would like for my father to understand I do not like it when he predicts negative things about me that are not true. He thinks he knows me well, but he does not. (The things that he thinks he knows about me are usually negative)

Age 31

I feel that my mother already understands everything about me because we talk often. She is always open to understand anything that I want or need to say to her.

Age 31

I would like for my parents to understand my voicing my opinion.

Age 32

I would like for my parents to understand that I am a free spirit and that no matter what happens, I am going to get my college degree and be successful. I am <u>really</u> trying.

Age 34

I would like for my parents to understand my independence. How I came to be so independent. My parents divorce caused the family to become distant and now that they both are remarried and at retirement age, they want <u>all</u> of their children to visit them as a <u>family unit</u> (on holidays) but, they do not understand that their divorce caused a "divorce" with the *whole family*.

Age 34

The one thing that I would want my parents to understand about me is that having both of them apart was and is very difficult for me. My parents separated and, as a result, my emotions and love for both of them seemed divided. As a result I think they never really fully understood my position—how it angered me and how I fought with dual emotions of love and anger. How, as an adult, these emotions have been resolved as all three of us now realize that love must be acknowledged regardless of whether the parents stay together or not.

Age 34

My mother still treats me like a little girl. I want her to understand that I am grown and that I have a family of my own now.

Age 35

I want my father to understand why I am so concerned about his drinking (alcohol). He does not seem to see a problem with it.

Age 35

I would like for my parents to understand who I am *today*. I feel that my parents treat me the same now as they did when I was younger. I have changed tremendously and I need my parents to understand my change and know that I have matured.

Age 35

I would like for my parents to understand that I am my own person (although I am their child) and I am able to move on in spite of the negative things that took place in my earlier years.

Age 37

I wish that when I tell my mom something (for example: about the children) that she would listen to the whole story before she begins to yell and get upset.

Age 37

I would like my mother to understand me as a person and learn to communicate with me. I wish she would learn to see the shortcomings that she possess rather than being so quick to be judgmental of others. If she begins to see this, then we can communicate better. Also, when I tell her that she shows favoritism towards my brother and sister over me, she tends to disagree.

Age 38

I would like for my parents to understand that I am a real person.

Age 40

I would like for my parents to understand that I would like to have a closer relationship with both of them. This is something that I have *never* had with them. I have a mom but I feel like I do not have one because we do not have a relationship at all. My dad has always been physically abusive to me and my mother.

Age 42

I would like for my parents to understand that the reason I am so over-independent is because of the way they brought me up. I feel that they should appreciate my independence.

Age 42

I would like for my parents to understand that I *do* change. My mom tends to act surprised when she notices a change in me. I want her to know that I *do* change and that I will *continue* to change. I will not stay the same as she may have remembered me the last time she talked to me.

Age 49

I really wish my parents understood how I *really* am

(how I feel).

Age 52

I would like for my mom to know me for who I am;

and to be more tolerant of the differences in our

lifestyles.

Age 53

I would like for my parents to understand that my

preferences and decisions do not always match their

ideal.

Resources for Parents

The New Strong-Willed Child
Dr. James Dobson

Bringing Up Boys
Dr. James Dobson

Bringing Up Boys Parenting Videos
Dr. James Dobson

Dare To Discipline
Dr. James Dobson

Love Must Be Tough
Dr. James Dobson

Preparing for Adolescence:
How to Survive the Coming Years of Change
Dr. James Dobson

Dr. James Dobson on Parenting
Dr. James Dobson

Parents' Answer Book
Dr. James Dobson

Night Light for Parents: A Devotional
Dr. James Dobson and Shirley Dobson

Life on the Edge
A Young Adults Guide to a Meaningful Future
Dr. James Dobson

ABOUT THE AUTHOR

Dr. Grace LaJoy Henderson is an Author, Publisher, Speaker, Workshop Facilitator, Motivator, Songwriter, and a Poet and has been writing since she was 13 years old.

She holds a PhD in Christian Counseling and a Bachelor's degree in Social Psychology. She has volunteer experience working with youth as a Sunday School Teacher, Vacation Bible School Teacher, Youth Leader, Youth Department Director, Children's Church Teacher, and Youth Drama Department Director. She also has professional experience working with youth and their families as a public school administrator.

Currently, Dr. Grace LaJoy Henderson conducts Writer's Breakthrough™ Workshops for writers and aspiring authors. Her writing has been featured in newspapers, on radio, and on television.

Her mission is to use her writing as a vehicle to educate, motivate, encourage, inspire, and most of all to minister!

The author welcomes your comments,

questions, and testimonies.

Inspirations by Grace LaJoy

P.O. Box 181

Raymore, MO 64083

E-mail address: poetry@gracelajoy.com

49

Books and Resources Available
by Dr. Grace LaJoy Henderson

Writer's Breakthrough: *Steps To*
Copyright and Publish Your Own Book
(Book and CD)

More Than Mere Words: *Poetry That Ministers*
(Christian Poetry Book)

Poetic Empowerment
(Spoken Word CD)

Poetic Book Series
Diversity in our Schools, Diversity in our Workplace
The Bad Butt Kids, He's Worth It, Our Employees...Our
Cornerstones

Understanding Each Other: *A Guide for Parents and*
their Children (Book)

In My Mama's House
(Book – ages 13-18)

How Can Jesus Be God?
(Children's Book)

Sex and the Young Woman: A Guide to Sexual Purity
(Book)

Blessed With A Gift *by Charmaine Jones*
(Poetry Book)

To learn more please visit us online at

www.gracelajoy.com or www.writersbreakthrough.com

Notes

Notes

Notes

Notes

Notes

Notes

Notes

Notes

Notes

Notes